CHAINS FORGED

IN FREEDOM

JYMI LIVESEY

DEDICATION

To my family, who have endured the distractions, long hours, and my absence from moments that mattered. Your patience and understanding made this journey possible.

To my wife, Lori, my sounding board, my support, and my best friend. Thank you for listening when I needed to vent and for standing beside me through it all. To my sons, Ayden, Keaton, and Jayce, who step up whenever I call and don't always hesitate to help when needed. Your willingness and support mean more than I can properly put into words.

To my father, who has passed, I'm sorry I wasn't around more. I hope this work makes you proud. To my mother and sister, who too often see less of us because of the demands of this path, thank you for your understanding and continued love.

To my friends Steve, Donny, Karen, Jackie, and Wayne, thank you for being there during overwhelming times and helping keep me grounded and moving forward. And to my coach, Jeanette, thank you for your patience, for standing by, and for doing your best to understand how my mind works.

None of this was built alone, even when it felt like it was.

Jymi

ACKNOWLEDGMENTS

This book wasn't written from a place of certainty or success. It came together through frustration, exhaustion, hard reflection, and the kind of moments where continuing forward feels uncertain at best.

Many of the thoughts in these pages were shaped during times when the answers weren't clear, and the path ahead didn't look promising. The conversations, experiences, and struggles shared by others along the way played a larger role in this book than they may ever realize. Honest discussions about failure, pressure, responsibility, and resilience helped give shape to ideas that might otherwise have remained unspoken. This book carries pieces of those realities within it.

To the people willing to speak honestly about what business, ambition, and responsibility truly cost, thank you for your openness. Truth has a way of cutting through isolation, and those moments of honesty matter more than success stories ever could. …And to anyone reading this who feels worn down, uncertain, or closer to their own breaking point than they expected to be, you're not the only one standing there. Sometimes strength isn't loud or inspiring. Sometimes it's simply waking up and choosing to continue one more day.

Thank you for reading.

ABOUT THE AUTHOR

James (Jymi) Livesey is an entrepreneur, business owner, and creative builder who has spent much of his life navigating the pressures that come with running a business and trying to build something meaningful from the ground up.

Through years of experience in business operations, marketing, and project development, Jymi has seen both the rewarding and the difficult sides of entrepreneurship. The long hours, responsibility, uncertainty, and personal sacrifices that often come with building a business became the foundation for the ideas explored in this book.

This book was written not from theory, but from lived experience. It reflects the realities of many business owners who quietly carry the weight of responsibility, the mental strain, and the moments where continuing forward feels harder than stopping.

Beyond writing, Jymi continues to work on creative and entrepreneurial projects, including business consulting, marketing development, and creative media production, including songwriting, music production, and working on an online radio station and community website. He lives in Ontario, Canada, with his family.

INTRODUCTION

Running a business isn't just work — it's war. And some days, it feels like the enemy is you.

One day, I woke up proud as hell to wear my logo. I built this brand. I created something from nothing. I felt strong, independent, like no boss in the world could ever hold a candle to the freedom I carved out for myself. That's the dream we all chase, right? Be your own boss. Build your own path. Fuck the system.

And then there are the other days—the ones where that same logo feels like a chain around my neck. When I look at the business I built, all I see is a jail cell of my own making. Deadlines that never end. Customers who bleed me dry. Bills that don't care if I sleep or not. I wonder if I've created my own hell, brick by brick, invoice by invoice.

That's the edge I live on. The edge between pride and despair. Between building a dream and collapsing under it. The edge where you start asking yourself the darkest

questions — the ones you don't say out loud because
people wouldn't understand.

This book isn't a motivational pep talk. It's not a "10
steps to get rich" guide. It's a survival manual. It's the
shit nobody talks about when they glorify
entrepreneurship on Instagram. I want to tell you the
truth — my truth — about what it actually feels like to
run a business: the wins, the breakdowns, the nights
staring at the ceiling wondering how the fuck you'll
make it through the week.

You'll read stories that come straight from my life. The
good, the bad, the moments I nearly broke. And
alongside those stories, I'll share what I've learned the
hard way — lessons and survival tools that might keep
you from falling as far as I did, or at least let you know
you're not alone when you hit bottom.

Because here's the reality: business isn't always glory.
Sometimes it's the edge of suicide. But it's also the edge
of becoming something stronger than you ever thought
you could be.

Bitter Pill #1 – You Are a Whore

The first thing in business you have to realize and accept is this: you are a whore.

You will do anything to make a buck. You are either fucking someone, or you're getting fucked. Period.

You might wear a three-piece Wall Street smile, or you might be the king of rock city — but underneath, you're still a whore. They say prostitution is the oldest business practice in history.

Guess what? They're right. Business is just selling yourself. Giving up your morals, bending your standards, doing whatever it takes to survive.

Do you have a problem with prostitution? Good. Now ask yourself why. Does your problem even make sense? Because if it does — if you think you're "above it" — you're in trouble. You may not have just stepped off the bus into the big city, but if you're reading this, you've already sold yourself, or you're about to.

Being a whore is a business. You give so you can take. You trade what you have — your time, your skills, your body, your mind, your energy — all for one thing: survival.

The world puts shame on prostitution because the powers-that-be don't want you to know the truth: you don't need to buy anything to make money. You just need to sell or use what you already have. Governments made it illegal because they can't tax what they can't see.

So here's the first bitter pill you need to swallow: Can you live with yourself? Can you look in the mirror and say out loud, "I am a whore.

Table of Contents

DEDICATION i

ACKNOWLEDGMENTS ii

ABOUT THE AUTHOR iii

INTRODUCTION iv

CHAPTER 1 The Rush of Creation...1

CHAPTER 2 Identity & Branding 6

CHAPTER 3 When the Logo Feels Like a Chain 15

CHAPTER 4 Self-Made Jail...26

CHAPTER 5 The Demise Mindset...35

CHAPTER 6 The Survival Mindset 43

CHAPTER 7 The Tools That Keep You Alive..53

CHAPTER 8 The Hollywood Ending.. 62

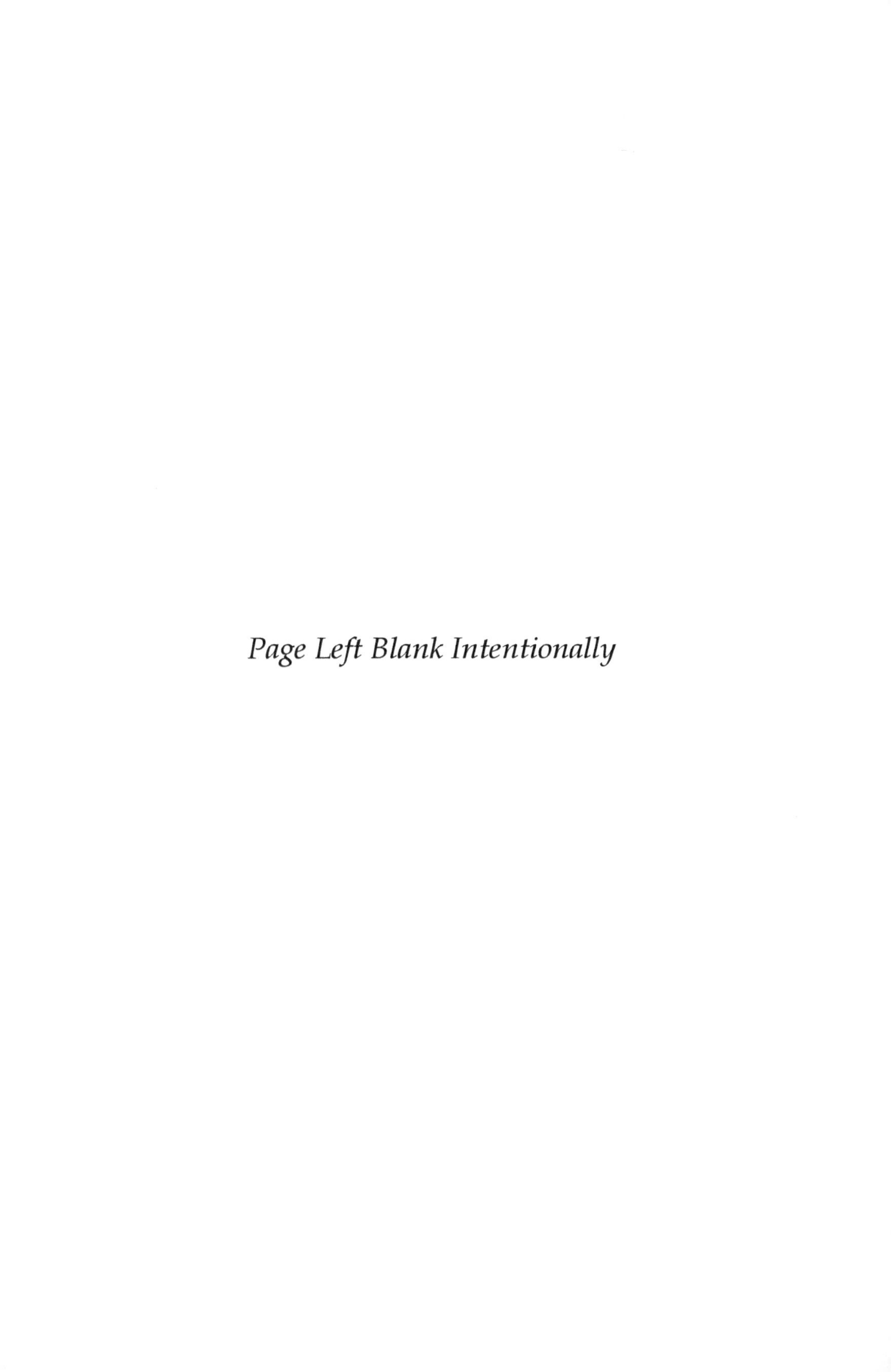

Page Left Blank Intentionally

CHAPTER 1

THE RUSH OF CREATION

Starting a business feels like a high. There's nothing else like it.

I remember the first time I saw my business name printed on something real — a logo on a shirt, a sign, a piece of paperwork. That shit hits harder than any drug. Suddenly, I wasn't just another guy working for someone else and collecting a paycheck. I was a creator. I was free.

The early days are pure adrenaline. Every little win feels huge. First customer? You feel like you're unstoppable. First cash transaction? You're holding proof that someone believes in what you built. You start dreaming about how big it can get, how you're going to dominate, how you'll never answer to a boss again.

You can't sleep because of excitement. Your head races with ideas, your phone notes fill up with plans, your mind doesn't shut down. You're in love with what you're building. You think about it in the shower, while you're driving, before you fall asleep, and the moment you wake up. It becomes oxygen.

That's the hook entrepreneurship sets deep into your skin and soul: you tasted freedom, and you can't go back. That rush — like cocaine — tricks you. You think this feeling will last forever, and I am unstoppable.

<u>Story – My First Big Win</u>

I'll never forget my first decent-sized job. It wasn't glamorous, but it was mine. I hustled hard, pitched it, got the "yes," and delivered. When I stepped back and looked at the finished work, I thought, "This is it. This is the moment my life changes."

I remember driving home after one of my first completed jobs, with a logo on my shirt, the kind of pride that makes you sit taller behind the wheel. It didn't matter that the profit was small. It didn't matter that the hours were long. I felt rich in a way a paycheck never gave me. I felt like I earned those cents more than I ever have before.

I blasted music the whole ride home while screaming the lyrics at the top of my lungs, already seeing the next ten years in my windshield — bigger shop, bigger clients, maybe employees running around while I sat back and ruled the empire.

That drive home, I was so proud, head high, logo on my shirt, can't wait to promise my family that the road ahead would be nothing but wins stacked on wins.

That night, I didn't sleep because I was buzzing, not from fear — from excitement. My mind was racing with possibilities. More jobs. Bigger projects. Maybe even hiring people. It felt like the world was opening up.

As always, a win comes with a loss, and sometimes you think you're the winner and wonder why people are booing or cheering for the other side. Well, that night, what I must have missed was the fog in the air. I didn't see the potholes. I didn't think about overhead. I didn't realize how many nights I'd be staring at a calculator, wondering how the fuck I'd make payroll or pay for supplies. In that moment, I only saw the dream.

And honestly? That's what kept me going. That first high — the rush of creation — it's the drug that hooks you long enough to endure what comes after.

The Lesson – Don't Get Drunk on the High

Don't get me wrong. Dreams are the creation and fuel. I am a dreamer. Without them, we have nothing. You must learn to control the dream, plan the adventure, and steer the ship.

Here's the truth: that freedom, that rush, is dangerous. It blinds you. You start thinking passion will carry you through everything. You ignore the cracks forming in the foundation—things like paperwork, cash flow, scheduling, taxes, and debt. You tell yourself, "I'll figure it out later. Right now, I just need to chase the next win. If I just do this now, I can collect more money."

But later and tomorrow always come. And when it does, all those cracks you ignored show up as sinkholes.

Starting a business is like falling in love. It's wild, it's euphoric, it makes you feel alive. But just like in relationships, passion fades and routines set in. When it does, you're left with the hard work of making it last.

So here's the takeaway: enjoy the rush, but don't trust it. It's fuel to get you moving, not the engine that will keep you alive, and remember every high has a crash.

This has become a staple in my life; the unfortunate part is that it has removed the excitement from my life. My wife constantly says, "He is as excited as he gets," and asks me, "Do you ever get excited anymore?" The answer is: I am excited deep inside; I can feel it burning there and wanting out, but now I am always looking for disappointment or the hurdle that will appear in front of me, blocking the path I need to figure out to get to the finish line. The finish line seems to be an infinite number of hurdles and circles.

CHAPTER 2

IDENTITY & BRANDING

<u>The Name</u>

My most successful business name carried my boys' initials. I chose that name for a few reasons, and every one of them mattered.

1. It opened the door to conversation.

People would always ask, "What do the initials stand for?" And when I answered, "They're my sons' names," the reaction shifted immediately. I wasn't just some guy hustling for a buck — I was a father, a family-first man, and that gave me instant credibility. Before I even sold a product, I had already sold trust.

2. It made the business personal.

That name was my family. It meant that every time I showed up, I was showing up for them. Food, shelter, clothes, life — everything I did was tied to those letters.

And when I felt like I couldn't keep going, when I was beat down and empty, the name itself pulled me back up. It reminded me why I was fighting in the first place.

3. It worked strategically.

One of those initials was an "A." That small detail pushed my business to the top of lists — back when the phone book mattered, and even now in search rankings. Never name your business with a "Z." Nobody finds you at the bottom of the pile. You don't want to be buried on page ten of Google or shoved in the back corner of a directory. You want to be seen first.

Identity in a Logo

Your business name matters. But so does your logo.

A lot of people think a logo is just a fancy picture, a little GIF or PNG you slap on invoices, websites, or social media. They couldn't be more wrong. A logo needs serious thought, because it's the symbol of your identity. It's what people remember when they forget everything else.

Here are the questions every entrepreneur should ask:

- Does it need to show what you do?
- Does it need words in it?
- Does it need multiple colors?

Most important: Can you wear it and display it with pride? Because if you can't stand behind your own logo, nobody else will.

The Controversial Example

This might get me in trouble, but I don't care — this is the truth: if you're someone who doesn't support the gay community, who feels their sexuality is tested every day, or you worry your sexuality might prevent you from doing business with your target market, then don't create a logo with a rainbow in it, or a blend of colours to look like a rainbow.

I'm not talking about politics here. I'm talking about survival. If your logo doesn't align with who you are, you won't stand behind it. If you can't defend it, wear it, and live with it, then it's the wrong logo for you.

A logo has to be believable. It has to be you. It has to further develop TRUST.

The Practical Side

Your logo should be recognizable instantly and visible at a distance. If it has words, make them clear and tied directly to your product, service, or name. Don't overcomplicate it.

And here's a design truth most people don't want to hear: keep your colors to a minimum. One color is best. Some people will argue, but one-color logos are usable everywhere. Multiple colors can get expensive to print, look messy in small formats, and be unreadable in black and white.

Think of the most iconic brands in the world. Their logos are simple, bold, and work in any environment. That's not an accident. That's strategy.

The Colour

As already stated, keep the colour simple, down to the least amount of colour you can. I am a firm believer in one colour, and you may get me to stretch to two – but it's a fucking hard pull.

Did you know there is science behind colours? If not, LEARN. Colours create moods, thoughts, feelings, and carry meanings. I will post just a taste of it here.

The Science of Colours in Marketing

Colours aren't just decoration — they mess with how people feel, focus, and buy. The brain processes colour faster than words, and each shade triggers an emotional response. Warm colours like red and orange spark urgency, excitement, and appetite (think sales tags or fast food). Blue builds trust and calm (banks, tech, healthcare use it to feel reliable). Green signals balance, nature, and money. Black screams luxury and power. Yellow grabs attention but can also cause anxiety if overused. Burgundy is commonly associated with and reserved for royalty. Look me up or guess what colour my logo is.

Branding – Get Your Name Everywhere

A name and logo don't mean shit if no one sees them. Branding is the act of shoving your identity into every corner of the world you touch. If you hand someone an invoice, your name better be on it. If you drive a truck, it should scream your brand from 100 feet away. Shirts, hats, pens, business cards, social media, websites, receipts — if it leaves your hand, it carries your mark.

Branding isn't a sucker punch from out in left field. Branding is a straight shot in the face, while standing in someone's way, making damn sure they notice you. It's about being so present, so visible, that people can't ignore you even if they want to.

And here's the truth: people don't remember you the first time they see your logo. Or the second. Or even the third. But by the tenth time, they know you. They may not know your face, but they'll recognize your brand. And that recognition is half the battle in business. Believe it or not, they may have never talked to you, seen your face, or known your name, but by the tenth time they see your logo, they will trust your brand because it is familiar to them.

It's not about being fancy — it's about being relentless. Every time someone sees your brand, they're reminded that you exist. You're in their head without being in the room. They will be thinking about what they need to talk to you about and why. That's how you win.

The biggest mistake entrepreneurs make is hiding their brand. They get shy about it, almost apologetic. Fuck that. If you can't stand loud behind your own brand, how do you expect anyone else to? Your brand has to be a persona.

So here's the rule: if you do something, anything, in your business, stamp your name on it. Own it. Wear it. Push it. Because a brand that isn't visible might as well not exist.

Your brand is a persona. It has to have a life of its own. Think of it like your best friend. If you wouldn't be seen in public with it, it's time to get a new friend.

And if you want proof of how far branding can go, study the rock band KISS. Gene Simmons is a branding genius — he's slapped that logo on everything from baby clothes to caskets. Love him or hate him, people notice. That's branding. Ohh…. and we in the KISS Army buy it all.

<u>The Lesson</u>

Your logo is more than design. It's your shield, your uniform, your handshake before you even open your mouth. If you treat it like decoration, you're already behind. If you treat it like your armor, you'll wear it with pride, and others will respect it.

Bitter Pill #2 – Your Brand Isn't Yours

Your brand isn't what you think it is. It's what other people think it is.

- If they see weakness, your brand is weak.
- If they see fake, your brand is fake. You don't get to decide — they do.

Your brand doesn't care about your feelings. It will either make you money or bury you in silence. And if the world ignores it, you don't have a business — you have a hobby.

CHAPTER 3

WHEN THE LOGO FEELS LIKE A CHAIN

There was a time I wore my logo like armor. Proud, tall, chest out. That logo meant I was building something, providing, creating my own life on my own terms. Even before I had a brick-and-mortar storefront, the logo was an entity. One that represented the business. Even though I owned and operated the business myself, it was more than just me. It was alive, its own being, to stand tall or fall.

But somewhere along the line, that same logo stopped feeling like armor and started feeling like a chain around my neck. What was once pride turned into a burden I couldn't put down. A captor that I could not escape.

I'd throw on the shirt in the morning, and instead of feeling energized, I felt trapped. My day wasn't mine anymore — it belonged to the brand. That shirt no longer said freedom. It said obligation. My truck was a moving billboard; it controlled how I drove, who I waved at and who I didn't, where I parked, and which streets I drove.

The Shift You Don't Notice

It doesn't happen all at once. That's the dangerous part.

At first, the pride keeps you blind. You don't realize how heavy it's getting because you're too busy celebrating every little win. Then, slowly, the weight builds. A bad customer. A mistake in production. A bad product. A bill you can't pay. A job that runs long and eats your entire weekend. You start waking up earlier, staying up later, sacrificing more and more of yourself to keep the wheels turning. Family starts making comments about not seeing you all week. Family making plans without you; if you can join, you join; if you can't, they expect it.

The logo becomes your leash. It follows you everywhere. You can't walk into a grocery store without someone saying, "Hey, you're the guy from…" and suddenly you're "on the job" again. You don't get just to be you anymore. You're always in the business. There's an old saying, "24/7, 8 days a week." It is so true, and you stop being you. You're now that guy, and they don't respect your time or life; they only see what you do or provide.

And that's when you start to notice the pride has curdled into pressure.

The Prison of Identity

When your logo becomes you, every failure feels personal.

It's not just "the business" that screwed up an order — you screwed it up. It's not just "the company" that took too long to reply—you failed. When people complain, they're not criticizing a brand. They're criticizing the person behind it.

It cuts deep because the logo you created to represent you becomes a mask you can't take off. It's glued to your face. People stop seeing the human and only see the brand.

And if the business stumbles, you don't just feel like you lost money — you feel like you lost yourself.

<u>PERSONAL INJECTION</u>

The one that fucking burns me the most is when people are impatient and want their stuff now.

I ran a successful business that specialized in custom work for clients. Each job was new, no cookie-cutter. Sure, I got faster at some things and slower at others because you're trying something new and it's taking three times longer than planned.

Customers, since the bullshit COVID lockdowns, have an Amazon attitude: "I ordered this yesterday, why is it not ready today?" … even when the quote indicates that the estimated delivery time is two weeks.

These same people would drop by my shop, call the shop, continuously interrupt the workflow and wonder what is taking so long. I was working 12–14 hours a day, 7 days a week. These same people would not be able to get a hold of me, as I was ignoring the door or phone to stay on production schedules, and they would say, "Well, if you worked more, I would not be waiting."

People would come in and say, "Wow, this must be a crazy time of year for you. You're looking burnt out. I hope you get some time off soon. Just wondering if my stuff is ready?" -- 8 FUCKING DAYS BEFORE THE EXPECTED DUE DATE.

The Smile That Hides the Bleeding

The logo demands you keep up front. You can't walk around with a business name on your chest and look broken. You can't tell clients, "I'm exhausted, I'm broke, I'm ready to snap." You smile. You shake hands. You say, "We'll take care of it."

Meanwhile, inside, you're crumbling. They walk away, and you drop your head on the table just hoping to rest, shut out the noise, or, if nothing else, for an early death, so your family can at least have your life insurance, if they can't have you.

You go home drained, sit in silence at the dinner table, and your family feels the distance. They don't understand why you can't just "leave work at work." But you can't. There's no separation anymore. The logo crawls into bed with you, whispers in your ear at 2 a.m., and drags you out of sleep with a dozen things you forgot to do.

It's the smile in public and the breakdown in private.

You're alone. Not even your family understands anymore. You made changes and promised them more time or money, but it didn't work out as planned. They don't see it, don't understand, or really don't want to know how the business is going or what it takes to run. Any conversation that comes close to the subject of money will either ignite RAGE or make you run and HIDE from any and all sounds.

I would frequently see the old art of Atlas, the Greek Titan, carrying the Earth. Always carrying it on his back and bent down on one knee as the weight is just too fucking much.

The Chain Reaction

Here's the fucked up truth: the business doesn't just own your workday. It starts with owning your life.

Vacations get skipped because you "can't afford" the time off. Family events get pushed aside because "the business comes first." Your marriage, your friendships, your health — they all take the hits.

And you start resenting it. The thing you once loved, the dream you once chased, now feels like a ball and chain you're dragging across broken glass. Your brain is split – you hope nothing ever goes wrong, and the other half wants to set it all on fire for a God damn break.

But walking away? That feels even worse. Because if you quit, you're not just shutting down a business — you're admitting defeat. You're telling the world the dream beat you. And deep down, you're telling yourself you weren't strong enough, and that everyone will be pointing, talking, and laughing.

So you keep dragging the chain.

<u>The Lesson – Learning to Carry the Weight</u>

This is the part nobody warns you about. They tell you about "the grind," but they don't tell you how it grinds you.

The pride that builds your identity can turn into the prison that suffocates you. If you don't build boundaries, systems, or ways to separate the human from the brand, the business will eat you alive.

Here's the truth: your logo is not you. It represents you, it works for you, but it is not you. If you don't learn that distinction, you'll drown under the weight of your own creation.

The chains never go away — every business you build ties you to new responsibilities. The trick isn't to avoid the chains. The trick is learning how to carry the weight without letting it drag you under.

By no means have I gotten this perfect for myself, but here are a few things I have implemented to give me and my family some peace of mind.

1) Work phone and personal phone are not the same and are not connected to each other in any way. When you leave the office, work cannot follow you. That person can learn to call within business hours or leave a message.

2) No email on your phone. Only set up email access on your desktop computer in the office. Yes, I said desktop—a laptop you can pick up and take home with you.

3) Set Alarms on your phone. I have one that tells me when to take a break for lunch and another that tells me, "GO THE FUCK HOME." It goes off at the end of the day, and I have promised myself to leave within 20 minutes of it going off. Enough time to put things away, save files and leave the work area ready for the next day.

4) I have even considered taking a small employment role elsewhere, forcing me to get away from my business, plus giving me the ability to show a bank that I work (BTW Banks hate the self-employed), a

guaranteed income that goes straight to my family for their needs.

5) Now exploring AI services to answer phones and emails…. Save that for another book.

Bitter Pill #3 – Freedom Has a Price

Freedom was the dream. The logo was your badge. But here's the truth: every business you build is another chain around your neck. Some chains are gold, some are rusted steel, but they all weigh the same. The question is — can you carry it without breaking? Can you carry them and your family at the same time?

CHAPTER 4
SELF-MADE JAIL

I thought starting a business was the great escape. I told myself, "No more bosses, no more rules, no more limits." But here's the ugly truth: I didn't escape shit. I just traded one kind of cage for a fucking another — and this time, I built the bars myself. Worse, if I tried to draw the roadmap out, I was in a cage built like Russian Dolls, one cage leading into another. Really, Russian Dolls with a bit of Snakes and Ladders built in. Land the attempt wrong, go backwards, or start again from the beginning.

The walls weren't built overnight. They stacked up slowly: bills, equipment loans, payroll, customers with endless demands, my own pride and ego that refused ever to admit weakness. My growing desire for a break, loneliness, and just wanting a day with my wife and boys.

Before I knew it, I wasn't free. I was an inmate, locked inside a system of my own creation.

The Illusion of Freedom

When you're an employee, you've got one boss. Maybe they're an asshole or worse Scottish, maybe not. Either way, when you clock out, you're done.

When you're self-employed, every customer is your boss. Every invoice and sales order is a new deadline, every "just a quick question" message is another manager breathing down your neck. You don't escape the 9-to-5—you upgrade to the 24/7, and as I said earlier, you work 8 days a week.

Lesson: Freedom without boundaries isn't freedom. It's chaos. If you don't build rules for yourself, you'll end up working harder, longer, and for less peace of mind than you ever did under a boss, and if not careful, for less profit meaning less money. Your family can lose you and your income.

My father passed away recently. I used to spend almost every weekend with him and my mother at our family home on our own little piece of paradise. The mud of the land I used to say was my blood. I felt recharged just walking on the grass. Since I took my business and expanded, I increased sales, customers, bills, demands, and headaches. I found myself not there. The few times I got there, I felt tense, as everyone else went swimming, boating, or just sitting in the shade with a drink. I sat uncomfortably thinking of what else I could, no… should be doing. What my week was going to look like, how money was going to move this week. I lost myself, I lost them, and now my dad forever. I was luckily there for him in his last moments of what consciousness he had. I can only hope he knew and knows that I am sorry.

I just want you to know and understand. A business is a beast, a living and breathing machine, and worse of all… a snowball. That bitch just keeps rolling and picking up more for you to do. I have never seen it melt away; it's always rolling and growing. Oh, and if you grew up with 4 full seasons, you know that a snowball can pick up shit, too…

<u>**The Jail Bars You Built**</u>

Every entrepreneur builds their own prison bars, one decision at a time:

- **Overhead:** Rent, insurance, payroll, equipment. That shop you dreamed of owning becomes a monthly noose.

- **Debt:** The loan for the truck, the credit line for supplies. Banks smiling when you sign the papers, waiting to crush you if you stumble.

- **Customer Expectations:** They want faster, cheaper, better — and you train them to expect it by never saying no.

- **Pride:** The deadliest bar of all. The one that says, "I can't quit. I can't admit I'm drowning. I have to prove I can handle it."

Each one feels harmless till you add them up. One little expense, one new client, one little promise. Over time, the bars close in.

<u>**Lesson:**</u> Be careful which bars you build. Some are necessary — but if you don't leave yourself a door, you'll self-suffocate in the cell you designed.

My wife and son want to purchase an investment property. One we can rent during the high times and use ourselves during the low. A place to get away that will pay for itself. A place for my 21-year-old son to start putting his money to work for him. The problem is that to do this, we need to pull equity loans, re-mortgage, and co-sign for him. Of course, this all falls on the year that I am behind on paperwork, haven't filed my taxes yet, etc. Banks already hate me as I am self-employed. They hate you more when you have any loose ends and do not understand timelines to make anything happen. The snowball hit me this year, exploded, and I am still digging my way out.

The Guard Inside Your Head

The worst part? You're not just the prisoner. You're the warden too.

You enforce the rules. You set the punishments. You're the one saying "one more hour, one more job, one more loan." Nobody else chained you to that desk at midnight — you did it to yourself.

And because you're both guard and inmate, there's no one to rebel against. You can't even blame someone else. You can't say, "fuck my boss," because the boss is you. That guilt cuts deeper than any outside pressure.

Lesson: Sometimes the bars aren't the real prison — it's the voice in your head telling you you're not allowed to rest, not allowed to stop, not allowed to fail. You have to fire that guard before you can breathe.

Here is an up-to-date story. I am sitting here writing this book, telling myself I want to get one more chapter out today, while I also have paperwork and quotes that need completing, a customer project that is due yesterday, and I feel like death. I have no energy; I just want to sleep. My eyes are burning; my heart feels like it quit. The smart thing is to stop and walk away. The guilt keeps me here pushing to my early grave, "GOD?!, Check please!"

It feels like the only way out is down.

The Emotional Cost

The jail doesn't just lock you in. It locks others out.

- Family starts to resent the business. They feel second place to "the brand."
- Friends stop inviting you because you're always "too busy."
- Days blur. You're not living — you're serving time.

You look out from inside your self-made cell and realize life is happening without you. That hurts worse than the money struggles.

Lesson: Business doesn't just steal time. It steals relationships if you let it. You have to decide what's worth being locked away from.

The Escape Question

When you realize you're in a jail of your own making, the obvious question hits: How do I get out?

You think about selling. About quitting. About burning it all down for a clean slate. But then you remember the debt, the bills, the pride. And even if you could walk away, would you? Or would you just build another jail somewhere else?

Sometimes escape isn't the answer. Sometimes survival is about breaking a few bars, opening some windows, and letting in air. Maybe you don't need to leave the jail — maybe you just need to stop being your own warden.

Lesson: Escape isn't always about quitting. Sometimes it's about carving out space to breathe inside the system you built.

The Lesson – You Built It, You Can Change It

Every entrepreneur builds some form of jail. That doesn't mean you're doomed to rot inside.

- Recognize the bars you built yourself.
- Break the ones that don't serve you.
- Stop being both the prisoner and the guard.
- And remember: the business exists to serve you — not the other way around. You'll always carry responsibility, but you don't have to live like an inmate.

<u>**Bitter Pill #4 – The Prison You Built**</u>

Most bankers, business coaches, and whatever they want to call themselves will tell you. Your problems and answers are in your cashflow. Fuck them… I have studied mine, rewritten it over and over. It doesn't matter. All it can help with is how much you must charge for your time to be profitable. It doesn't cap the time it calculates, nor does it make space for sleeping, eating, friends, family, and yourself. Fucking right, I put me at the end of this list, and that is the first and biggest mistake.

You must think of yourself first, with you at the top of the list, and include family and friends too. Fuck everyone and everything else.

You have all heard of Count Dracula. Life is the true vampire. Like currency, time is gold.

CHAPTER 5

THE DEMISE MINDSET

There comes a point where you don't dream anymore. You don't even fight. You just sit in the shop, or the truck, or your office, staring at the walls of your own making and wondering if burning it all down would hurt less than dragging it on for one more day. On those really dark days, you wonder if your family would be better off if you were dead, let them collect life insurance, sell your shit, and have a better life.

This is the Demise Mindset. It's the place where exhaustion turns into collapse, and where survival feels like a joke you're not laughing at anymore. It doesn't always mean death, though some days it feels that close. Sometimes it's literal — dark thoughts creeping in. Sometimes it's business suicide — the urge to torch the whole fucking thing just to finally breathe.

The demise mindset isn't one big breakdown. It's a slow slide, and you don't even notice until you're already at the bottom. For every foot you slide, it's a mile to go back up.

The Symptoms of Collapse

Here's what it looks like when you're slipping into it:

- **Numbness**. Wins don't feel like wins anymore. That customer who used to make you proud? Now they're just another demand. You stop celebrating anything.

- **Short fuse**. Family says one wrong word, and you snap. Customers get the fake smile, then you rage when they leave.

- **Obsession**. You replay mistakes over and over, ignoring the fact that you've done a hundred things right. One fuck-up becomes your whole identity.

- **The fantasy of escape**. You catch yourself thinking about quitting, walking away, selling it all, or disappearing. Not planning — just imagining it like a guilty pleasure.

<u>**Lesson:**</u> If you catch yourself here, it's not weakness. It's a warning light. Ignore it, and the engine seizes. Though I didn't, you need to swallow your pride now and ask for help. Do this before the vultures wake and circle. Once they fly above your head, they will not leave until you are dead.

The Lies You Tell Yourself

The demise mindset feeds on lies. They sound like motivation, but they're poison.

- "If I just work harder, it'll fix itself."
- "My family will understand once I succeed."
- "It's just a rough patch, I'll push through."
- "If I quit now, I'll be a failure forever."

…. And there are a million more variations of self-hate and self-cheering.

Every one of those lies keeps you chained to the wheel. They turn guilt into fuel, but that fuel is acid. It eats you from the inside out. An acid-reflux that you cannot cure and a burn you do not feel till it breaks the skin.

<u>**Lesson**</u>: The hardest truth in business is this —
pushing harder doesn't always save you. Sometimes it
buries you.

<u>The Dangerous Edge</u>

This is the edge in the title. The edge of suicide — not
just death, but destruction.

- Some business owners think about ending their own
  lives.
- Others commit business suicide — walking away,
  letting it burn, watching the dream collapse.

The edge feels seductive. You start thinking: "What if I
just stopped?" Not slowed down. Didn't take a break.
Just… stopped.

And the scariest part? On the outside, nobody sees it.
You're still smiling in public. You're still shaking hands.
You're still the logo, the brand, the owner who "has it all
together." Inside, you're dying.

I was staring at the edge of the blade… cut me or cut
it.

I had banks and others calling for money, customers wanting projects completed, suppliers delaying shipments… it couldn't get any worse. I was, by nature, already beginning to hide from it all. I went home, spent a night with my family, and said nothing. I came back to the office the next morning and made my decision. I loved my family, and this business wasn't worth them, so I chose to cut the business and risk business suicide. Fuck who I owe money to, fuck every customer trying to reach me. (I should add that I owed nothing to any customer at this point; somehow, I got the work out first.)

Took a physical and mental break. Once I felt I could think clearly, I looked at my cash flow projections. I took a long, hard look at the services I offered and the profit margins per service. From that, I found how much I need to make each month to survive and rebuild. I also saw that I could raise prices on some items and completely drop others that were too long to produce and had varying profit margins. Dialed it in and went back to work.

Though very hard, you need to step away, step back, take another look.

(I will also add that I am writing this book while still running the business, and the results of this trial are still unknown. I only hope that I chose right, and did not miss the exit I maybe should have taken)

Survival vs. Demise

Here's the line you have to learn to see:

- **Demise Mindset**: Isolation. Exhaustion. Guilt. Shame. Obsession with failure. Fantasies of escape.
- **Survival Mindset**: Honesty. Boundaries. Asking for help. Remembering you exist outside the fucking business.

Lesson: You don't avoid the demise mindset by working harder. You survive it by cutting the lies and choosing yourself over the grind.

You may not be able to do this alone. Seek a business coach. Yes, they cost money, but they are people you have to let in and help you see in the dark and through the fog.

The Lesson – Choosing Survival

- Recognize the symptoms. Don't numb them out with more work.
- Stop lying to yourself. Harder isn't always better.
- Talk to someone. A friend, your spouse, a fellow business owner, or a coach. Silence is gasoline on the fire.
- Remember the business exists for you — not the other way around.

This isn't motivational bullshit. This is survival. If you don't choose survival, the demise mindset will choose for you. And it doesn't give a fuck if you live through it.

Bitter Pill #5 – Quitting Isn't Always Weakness

Sometimes quitting is survival.

If you have already quit in your mind and you are finding comfort in that, then fucking quit. Run, Forest Run, and keep running. This wasn't for you.

Sometimes shutting the doors is the only way to stay alive. Don't let pride be the reason you die in silence. Don't let business run you into the grave and away from your family…run it or KILL IT!!!

CHAPTER 6
THE SURVIVAL MINDSET

There's a point where you've stood on the edge long enough that you either fall or you find a way to live with the fuckin dead of space staring back at you. That's survival. In the moment you find a path you are comfortable with, you will once again feel calm, in power, and ready… that is, until someone asks you what's going on and when you tell them, they twist their face and look at you like you've just pissed your pants while pumping your own chest.

I've seen both sides of it. The dark days were the only thing keeping me moving, whether it was guilt, fear, or straight stubbornness. And the days when I caught myself before sliding too far — where I forced myself to stop, step back, and say, "This business exists for me, not the other way around."

The survival mindset isn't about winning. It's not about crushing sales, scaling, or becoming the next Elon Fuck-Face Musk. It's about staying alive in one piece long enough to keep playing and paying.

Dead men don't build empires, and burned-out owners don't keep their families fed.

Rebuilding After the Crash

If you've hit bottom, you already know: the climb back up is brutal. But it's also where you learn the most. You learn what you're made of, and if you have finally let your family in on the details, you learn what they are made of and what they think of you.

Survival looks like:

- Cutting dead weight services that drain you dry --- CASH FLOW IS A MUST
- Raising prices on the stuff that actually makes money --- PROFIT AND LOSS ANALYSIS
- Saying "NO" to customers who expect Amazon speed when you're a one-man shop.

- Taking a break without apologizing. --- FUCK EVERYONE AND FIX YOU FIRST

The first step is admitting the old version of your business is dead. That dream you started with? Fuck it, it's gone.

What rises next is leaner, sharper, and built for you — not just for survival, but for sanity, and may look different than you ever imagined.

Redefining Success

You want to know the biggest lie in business? That success has a universal definition. It doesn't.

For some, success is millions in the bank and countless employees. For me, success is food on my family's table, bills paid, time on the water, and the ability to tell a customer to fuck off if they cross the line.

The survival mindset demands you stop measuring your life by other people's fake fucking public persona. You have no idea of their truth, just as they don't know yours.

You don't need to scale. You don't need to dominate the market. You need to live. If your business feeds your life instead of draining it, that's SUCCESS!!.

Boundaries or Bust

Survival means building walls. Not against opportunity, but against the cancer that eats you alive: overwork, guilt, and endless customer demands.

- **Phone Boundaries**: Separate work from personal. If you're reachable 24/7, you're a slave.
- **Time Boundaries**: Alarms that tell you when to leave the shop. Not suggestions — orders.
- **Mental Boundaries**: Recognize when the guilt in your head is the warden talking, not you. Fire him.

Boundaries aren't a weakness. They're life support. Without them, you'll drown.

Family First, Business Second

Here's a bitter truth: no one ever lies on their deathbed wishing they had answered more emails. They wish they had more time with their kids, their partner, and their friends.

If your business is costing you your family, you're not surviving — you're bleeding out. Make choices that put them first. Your logo won't sit at your funeral. Your kids will. Your logo won't hug you and tell you it loves you — your kids will, and if you're lucky, your beautiful wife will too.

So, what the fuck did I do?

Well, I looked at my cash flow, right down to the number of billable hours I could produce each day. Billable hours. Remember, you can't bill your time for doing your books, inventory, marketing, training, on the phone, answering emails, writing quotes, writing invoices, sweeping your floors, etc. Nothing but pure production is billable.

What I found was that my business grew to an impressive level, and the bottleneck is production. Being a one-man show was what was killing me. So, I hired someone. Paid them close to 40K in their first year. They assisted on jobs that brought in roughly 60K. Yahoo 20K profit, I was rocking it…. Until customers started coming back, as the quality wasn't good. Lifelong customers weren't buying if my employee was doing any of the work. I had to make the decision to sever ties. This alone didn't stop the bleeding; people kept coming back. Of the 60K in sales the employee helped with, I had to throw out materials and remake roughly 40K of product. So in the end, my well-thought-out option for survival cost me 80K in expenses, with 20K Profit, leaving me with a 60K death scar.

Not going to lie, that took some wind out of the sales. I then, by default, went back to blindly working and collecting as much money as I could until I hit a new level of burnout. A burnout so bad I could feel my heart beat, my joints stiffen, my head ache, and my thoughts run rampant.

What did I do… well, I have gone a whole new way. I have decided to take a brain break. Though not completely. I took a job with another company for a guaranteed paycheck, working 40 hours a week, Monday to Friday. Closed my business doors and opened by appointment in the evenings.

So now I am working 8 hours a day at some place, doing what I do there. Returning to my business after work and working there for 4 hours a night, Monday to Wednesday, and 6 hours on Sunday. (Not like I was going to fucking church anyway, what a joke…. That's another book.) Here's the weird part. I am working 58 to 60 hours a week, but my time at my own business is short. I am getting stuff done, but because it's a short time there, the time flies by. I am not stressed while I am there, and I am paying bills. I think this may work and will continue to work. The more debt I pay down, the more time I will be able to spend with my family.

So you never know where a decision or information will take you. But I do know that if you don't stop and look both ways, your business is going to run you down like a raccoon on the highway taking on a semi-truck.

The Lesson – Survival Is Winning Enough

The survival mindset isn't glamorous. Nobody's posting about it on Instagram. It's quite wins:

- Saying no without guilt.

- Eating dinner at home three nights in a row.
- Taking a day off and watching your kid's game.
- Paying the bills without losing your mind. That's winning. That's enough.

<u>Bitter Pill #6 – Enough Is the Goal</u>

You don't need to be the richest, biggest, fastest, or most famous. You need to survive. Enough money. Enough time. Enough peace of mind.

Chasing "more" forever is what drives you to the edge. Learning to say "enough" is what pulls you back.

Learning that your biggest investment and richest gem are the people in your house who call you DAD or MOM, and the spouse who smiles when you come home, lays with you, kisses you goodnight, and whispers that they love you.

<u>Conclusion</u>

Business: The Edge of Suicide. Sorry for the title and darkness, but you need to know the hardships and the mental anguish. This is not in textbooks, it's not taught, you have to live it to know it and relate.

Trust me, there are many times that I have pictured my death, felt the noose, pictured that head-on crash with a tree, the deep cliff at the side of the road... many, many times.

Run your business, do not let it run you.

Keep your family close and tell spoiled customers to FUCK OFF.

CHAPTER 7

THE TOOLS THAT KEEP YOU ALIVE

Mindset keeps you standing. But numbers keep you breathing.

You can have all the pimp-strut in the world, but if the math doesn't work, you're fucked.

Most business owners avoid the numbers. They "mean to" do books, they "plan to" make a budget, but instead, they just keep pushing forward and praying it works out. That's how you die. Never count on a prayer. There are a lot of dead people who waited for God to save them.

This chapter is blunt, boring, and absolutely necessary. You don't need an accounting degree — you just need to understand the basics enough to know when you're winning or when you're digging your grave.

Tool 1: Cash Flow – Your Business Lifeline

Cash flow is the timing of money. Not profit.

Just what's coming in vs. what's going out — and when.

Why it matters:

- You can look profitable on paper and still go bankrupt if bills are due before payments land.
- Customers love to pay late. Banks don't.

How to build it (simple):

Week/ Month	Cash In (Payments)	Cash Out (Bills)	Net Movement	Balance
Week 1	$3,000	$2,000 (supplies, rent)	+$1,000	$1,000
Week 2	$0 (waiting on invoices)	$1,500 (insurance, utilities)	-$1,500	-$500
Week 3	$5,000	$2,500 (payroll, materials)	+$2,500	$2,000
Week 4	$2,000	$2,000 (loan, misc)	$0	$2,000

Watch the dips. If you don't know when you'll be negative, you're already fucked.

Tool 2: Profit & Loss (P&L) – The Truth Teller

Cash flow tells you when you run out.

P&L tells you if you're actually making money.

Simple breakdown:

Revenue	Amount
Sales (Jan)	$20,000
Total revenue	$20,000

Expenses	Amount
Materials & Supplies	$7,000
Labor (if employees)	$4,000
Rent & Utilities	$2,000
Marketing	$1,000
Insurance	$500
Misc	$500
Total Expenses	$15,000

Net Profit (Revenue – Expenses) = $5,000

If that number is negative for more than a couple of months, you're bleeding out.

<u>Tool 3: Budget – Your Fence Against Chaos</u>

A budget isn't prison. It's a fence that keeps you from walking into traffic.

Steps:

1. Write down all fixed costs (rent, insurance, phone, internet).
2. Add variable costs (supplies, gas, shipping).
3. Add debt payments.
4. Add your own pay (yes, you count).

Basic layout:

<u>Category</u>	<u>Monthly Budget</u>	<u>Actual Spent</u>	<u>Difference</u>
Rent/Utilities	$2,000	$2,000	$0
Supplies	$3,000	$3,500	-$500
Marketing	$500	$300	+$200
Insurance	$300	$300	0
Owner Pay	$2,000	$0 (oops)	+$2,000

Looks great at $2,200 forward carrying balance; however, if "Owner Pay" is always zero, you don't have a business—you have a hobby that's killing you.

That $2000, now mistakenly treated as profit, is debt your family now has, as you didn't provide it.

<u>**Tool 4: Break-Even Point – Your Survival Number**</u>

This is the minimum sales you need to make to not lose money.

<u>**Formula:**</u>

Fixed Costs ÷ (Price – Variable Cost) = Break-Even Units

<u>**Example:**</u>

- Fixed Costs (monthly overhead) = $5,000
- You charge $500 per job
- Materials/Labor per job = $200
- Profit per job = $300
- $5,000 ÷ $300 = 17 jobs to break even

Simple … Everything past 17 jobs is profit. Everything below = debt.

You need to pay close attention to this when you have varying profits per job and variable costs.

Bitter Pill #7 – Numbers Don't Lie

You can bullshit yourself about being "busy." You can convince yourself that customers "love you." But numbers don't give a shit about your feelings.

- If cash flow says you're short, you're short.
- If P&L says you're losing money, you're losing money.
- If your budget says you're broke, you're broke.

Your pride won't pay rent. Your logo won't cover payroll. Numbers don't lie. Look at them, or they'll bury you.

I don't mean once a year. Look at the numbers every fucking month or weekly if you can. I visit my cash flow often and have added a few extra columns to my cash flow that I go back and fill in; therefore, I am using one sheet to do my cash flow and budget, with actual spending for tracking.

<u>**The Lesson: Numbers = Survival**</u>

- Track your cash flow weekly.
- Review P&L monthly.
- Build and adjust a budget quarterly.
- Know your break-even point like you know your kids' birthdays.

If you hate numbers, too bad. Hate them with your accountant, hate them with a bottle of whiskey, hate them while you scribble on a napkin. Just don't ignore them.

Because every entrepreneur who died on the edge of suicide had one thing in common: they weren't looking at the numbers until it was too late.

Neglect is a crutch, a calculator is your shield, and the pen can be your friend or the knife that you see with your last breath.

CHAPTER 8

THE HOLLYWOOD ENDING

Like all the bullshit that comes out of Hollywood — every tear-jerking story where the star starts mediocre, starts something new with a smile, disaster strikes, everyone prays they'll make it, and somehow they do. The money rolls in, the family hugs, and the camera fades into a fucking sunset…

I AM DOING FUCKING FINE. MY LIFE IS FUCKING GREAT.

I HAVE ALL THE MONEY I NEED. MY BILLS ARE ALL PAID.

Sorry. That's all bullshit.

I'm still working my ass off to rebuild what fell apart. Plugging leaks I didn't even know existed. I'm not smiling, my family doesn't have all the answers, and no — we're not posing for a fucking Hallmark ending.

But we're unified. We're pushing forward. We've made changes, and we're crossing our fingers that they were the right ones.

This book wasn't written to glorify failure or preach success. It's written to help you see the death pits I fell into — so maybe you can walk around them instead of through them.

A million "experts" will say I don't know what I'm talking about. They're wrong. I'm not a trust-fund philosopher or some fake motivational prick on TikTok.

I'm in the trenches, fighting for survival.

If this book helped you, please tell me.

If it didn't—tell me that, too. I can only keep learning.

Whatever you do, don't let this book kill your dream. That was never the point. I'm a dreamer. I believe in dreams. I just want you to dream without dying for it.

Because one day, you might find yourself standing on the same sharp edge I did — staring into the dark, feeling cold and alone at 1 am.

If that day comes, remember this: the decision is yours.
The control is yours.

Don't let this fucked-up world or some three-piece-suit
asshole push you off.

Love from the trenches — we can survive.

The evil can be defeated.

JYMI LIVESEY